A STUDENT'S GUIDE TO
PSYCHOLOGY

ISI GUIDES TO THE MAJOR DISCIPLINES

GENERAL EDITOR

JEFFREY O. NELSON

EDITOR

JEREMY BEER

A Student's Guide to Psychology

DANIEL N. ROBINSON

ISI BOOKS
WILMINGTON, DELAWARE

The Student Self-Reliance Project and the ISI Guides to the Major Disciplines are made possible by grants from the Philip M. McKenna Foundation, the Wilbur Foundation, F. M. Kirby Foundation, Castle Rock Foundation, J. Bayard Boyle, Jr., the Huston Foundation, the William H. Donner Foundation, Pierre F. and Enid Goodrich Foundation, and other contributors who wish to remain anonymous. The Intercollegiate Studies Institute gratefully acknowledges their support.

Cataloging-in-Publication Data

Robinson, Daniel N.
        A student's guide to psychology / Daniel N. Robinson.
        1st ed.—Wilmington, DE : ISI Books, 2002.

        p. ; cm.

        Includes bibliographical references.
        ISBN 1-882926-95-1
        1. Psychology. I. Title.

BF121   .R63   2002   2002107926
158—dc21   CIP

Published in the United States by:

        ISI Books
        Post Office Box 4431
        Wilmington, DE 19807-0431

                Cover and interior design by Sam Torode
                Manufactured in Canada

CONTENTS

INTRODUCTION

❧

PSYCHOLOGY, that "nasty little subject," as William James called it, embraces the full range of actions and events which appear to depend, at least in part, on perceptions, thoughts, feelings, motives, and desires. These very processes, however, also seem to depend, at least in part, on internal biological states as well as external social influences. To complicate matters even further, influences can be "social" only insofar as they are perceived or thought of as such, and can only be "influences" to the extent that they converge on motives, feelings, and desires. These considerations, in turn, reflect or are in some way conditioned by larger cultural and historical influences. In all, then, what James ironically described as a "nasty little subject" is in fact a complex and overarching set of problems and perspectives arising from the abiding project of self-knowledge.

That project, of course, is not *owned* by any discipline or society of scholars or scientists. Self-knowledge includes factors at once biological, genetic, anatomical, medical, social, civic, political, moral, aesthetic—the full range of facts and endeavors that give shape, direction, and definition to a given life. There can be no sharp line establishing just where the psychological domain ends and another begins. Typically, specialists in one domain assume to be more or less settled what those in another accept as a central problem or question. Thus, the political scientist accepts Aristotle's dictum that "man is a social animal," and then proceeds to examine the various forms and foundations of political community. The evolutionary biologist might examine the adaptive advantages conferred by social life; the psychoanalyst, the consequences of withdrawal from the social context.

The history of science leaves no doubt but that such specialized modes of inquiry yield a rich crop of useful facts and basic principles by which to understand a wide range of phenomena. Equally clear, however, is that these gains are not without cost. The principal cost is the narrowing of perspective and the tendency to regard a small part of the overall picture as revealing the essential nature of the whole. The biochemist who accurately summarizes the atomic and molecular composition of the human body has not summarized anything of interest about the human *person* whose body it is. The neurophysiologist who presents an account of the processing of information in the optic nerve does not explain just what makes one scene breathtaking and another prosaic. Needless to say, responsible biochemists and neurophysiologists claim no more than what is warranted by the findings of rigorous research and what seem to be plausible inferences. But the unsuspecting consumer of information, especially when encouraged by the specialist's exaggerated claims, is vulnerable to the "nothing but" fallacy: Optic nerve discharges are essential to normal vision, therefore vision is *nothing but* these discharges!

The sections that follow present findings and theories developed within specialized fields of psychology and kindred disciplines. Reminders are supplied regularly to the effect that these findings and theories form some part of the larger story, but surely not the whole story. Moreover, it can only be the more complete story that allows one to decide finally just how important the various parts of the tale are. Consider, for example, a story such as *King Lear* or *War and Peace*. If these are taken in their wholeness, it becomes clear that the essence of the stories would be unaffected had Lear been a Dutch rather than a British king, or if Pierre had not been quite as tall. The point can be expressed economically: Until one has a defensible and general conception of the essence of human nature, all attempts to establish any one *part* of the story as essential must be premature.

This much granted, it is also clear that what we might come to regard as the "essential" nature of anything must include its composition, its functioning, and the ways in which it manifests itself. It would be odd to discuss the essential nature of human beings, for example, while having no basis whatever on which to classify something as "human"; or to assert that an essential feature of such beings is "thought," but with no clear identification of actions or events as instances of "thought." Though the parts of the story are insufficient, they are nonetheless vitally important if there is to be progress toward the fuller account.

PHILOSOPHICAL PSYCHOLOGY: INVENTING THE SUBJECT

Ancient Greece (again)

Gnothe se auton ("Know thyself") is the maxim carved into the temple at Delphi honoring Apollo. It is to the world of ancient Greece that one must look for the origins of psychology as a subject of study, a discipline holding out the promise of knowledge. It is to this same world that one turns when considering most of the subjects with which the scientific and scholarly worlds are concerned. Why is this so? The reasons generally offered are many, none of them entirely successful. The thesis that explains the cultural achievements of Hellenism as the result of a slave economy permitting the wealthier class to engage in intellectual pursuits proves to be empty. Slave economies before and after the age of classical Greece yield no comparable record, nor are the greatest intellectual accomplishments of ancient Greece those of the aristocracy. Indeed, those who may be said to have founded philosophical inquiry were Greek colonists in Asia Minor, removed from

---

PYTHAGORAS (c. 580–c. 500 B.C.) was the first to call himself "philosopher." He is credited with dazzling discoveries in mathematics and with the discovery of the mathematical principles of music. His teachings were also influential in shaping some of the main tenets of Platonic thought. Little is known about the life of Pythagoras; he himself, like Socrates, wrote nothing. It appears that he was originally from the island of Samos and later founded an academic society in Kroton (in southern Italy), which was at one and the same time a sort of religious community and scientific school, and which had many devoted followers. He was eventually forced to flee from Kroton to Metapontion, where he later died.

the wealthier centers of the Greek mainland.

A more promising if inevitably incomplete explanation draws upon the nature of ancient Greek religion. The world of the Hellenes was pious, but there was no *official* religion; no set of constraining orthodoxies; neither priests nor gods in possession of "The Truth." What the gods of Olympus enjoyed was an immortality combined with formidable physical powers. None of them was endowed with omniscience, and few of them—and these only occasionally—took any special interest in the humble affairs of mere mortals. On the dilemmas that mark out the subject matter of psychology, philosophy, and the natural sciences, the gods of the ancient Greek world were silent, if not ignorant.

It is said that Pythagoras of Samos (c. 580–c. 500 B.C.) was the first to call himself a *philosopher*—a friend (*philos*) of wisdom (*sophos*). Pythagoras surely was not the first person to raise the questions that still animate philosophical discussions, nor was the Greek-speaking world the first world to come to grips with personal, moral, and social problems. There is ample evidence in the records of older cultures—Mesopotamian, Oriental, Egyptian, Hebrew—of serious thought about such matters. One turns to the world of ancient Greece, therefore, not to locate the date on the calendar when problems of a certain kind first appeared, but to locate the period in which such problems were first subjected to the sustained, critical, and skeptical modes of analysis that continue to characterize philosophy as a distinct subject.

Central to this mode of analysis is the suspension of belief in the authority of tradition, revelation, or the individual. To address a problem in a philosophical manner is to acknowledge that neither revealed truths nor the mere customs of a people, let alone the alleged wisdom or inspiration of some person within the community, can be the last word on any fundamental issue. Understood in these terms, philosophy is the foundation on which other and

---

HIPPOCRATES (c. 460–c. 377 B.C.) was the founder of an influential school of medicine situated on the island of Cos, in Greece. Based on direct studies of patients, Hippocrates concluded that the perceptual, motor, and cognitive functions are controlled by the brain (and not the heart, as was commonly believed). Rejecting nonphysical explanations of illness, he was the first physician to accurately describe the symptoms of diseases like epilepsy and pneumonia, and his curative recommendations generally relied on factors that promoted natural healing: fresh air, a good diet, exercise, etc. The followers of Hippocrates wrote more than sixty books on a wide range of medical topics, and his school of medicine required students to take the ethical oath that now bears his name.

similarly disciplined modes of inquiry—other *disciplines*—were developed, especially the natural sciences.

Before the birth of philosophy as a discipline, one looked to the seer, the oracle, the poet for guidance and for insight into the human condition. The figure most regularly consulted in the Greek world was the blind bard Homer (fl. c. 700 B.C.), whose epic songs, the *Iliad* and the *Odyssey*, record the full range of human passions and powers, and the manner in which their deployment leads to triumph or disaster. Within these works is a skeletal "psychology": Life comes about through the presence of a kind

---

PLATO (427–347 B.C.) is author of those dialogues that established the very terrain of philosophical speculation: the problems of knowledge, of ethics, of politics. His Academy would be rich enough in its offerings to retain Aristotle as a student for nearly twenty years. An Athenian aristocrat, Plato was originally named Aristocles, but his broad shoulders earned him his nickname, which derived from "platon," meaning "broad." After the execution of his teacher Socrates in 399 B.C., Plato visited various Greek cities in Africa and Italy, gaining exposure to the ideas of Pythagoras. In 387 B.C. he returned to Athens and founded the Academy (an institution that remained in operation until A.D. 529, when it was closed by Emperor Justinian). Sometime in the 360s B.C. Plato traveled to Syracuse to tutor Dionysius II, the new king of that city-state, hoping to make of him the sort of philosopher-king he believed to be the ideal ruler. But the effort was a spectacular failure, and Plato returned, with some difficulty, to Athens. There he died in his sleep at around the age of eighty after attending a student's wedding feast.

of air (*pneuma*) and soul (*psyche*), with emotion and motivation impelled by events in the heart and chest or throat. There is a "soul" that may leave but return to the body, bearing the contents of a dream; there is a "soul" that, once lost, leaves only death in its wake. As with the great poets and dramatists of every age and culture, Homer provides an account of the human condition that cannot be gleaned either from philosophical or scientific study. But it remains a *poetic* account and, as such, raises a score of questions for each one it seems to settle.

Socrates and Plato

Thus did the early philosophers of the Greek-speaking world initiate wide-ranging speculation on the nature of reality, of the heavens, of matter itself. But it is with Socrates (470–399 B.C.) that the focus of philosophical inquiry shifts from inanimate nature to human nature. It is with Socrates that *psychological* problems receive their first clear definition, their first provisional solutions. Broadly classified, these are the *problem of knowledge*, the *problem of conduct*, and the *problem of governance*. Consider first the problem of knowledge: How is it that one can know anything? What is the mark or sign of true knowledge? What means are available by which it can be gained? How can one be sure that one is not simply deluded or hallucinating? Where two incompatible claims about what is "known" come into conflict, how is the difference to be resolved? Is there a difference between knowledge and belief? Knowledge and opinion?

Within the discipline of philosophy, questions of this sort form a special field of inquiry known as *epistemology*, an account or a study (*logos*) of knowledge (*episteme*). These same questions are psychological in that they address such fundamental processes as perception, cognition, learning, memory, judgment, belief. Socrates, it seems, wrote nothing; rather, he staged debates with one or another friend, one or another philosopher, testing the arguments of each and laying down challenges by which to show their errors and inconsistencies. The record of these encounters survives in that most foundational of all philosophical writing, Plato's *Dialogues*. In these, the genius of Socrates and Plato (427–347 B.C.) are merged, as the latter reconstructs and creates whole dramas of inquiry on the broadest and deepest of issues. Although there is no single and entirely stable "solution" to the problem of knowledge, the development or various stages of Socrates' thought on these matters can be reduced to several core principles:

A. Behind the ever-changing and cluttered facts of the perceptible world there is the realm of the unchanging, and it is in this realm that truth is to be found. The evidence for this is provided by mathematics. Whereas any physical or drawn figure with three sides and one right angle can only approximate the true form of a rectilinear triangle, the Pythagorean theorem discloses just this true form. Perceptible triangles come and go; the true form of the triangle is immutable and eternal.

B. In light of (A), the knowledge gleaned by the senses must be tentative, uncertain, changeable. The knowledge worth having is not discovered "out there," but recovered from within the mind's own resources. Pythagoras did not discover the theorem that bears his name by looking at three-sided figures, but by reflecting deeply on the nature of things. The truths of mathematics are truths contained within the "soul" itself, reached by way of philosophical guidance.

What Socrates' thesis asserts, in contemporary terms, is that the comprehension of abstract truths is based on essentially *rational-cognitive* processes rather than those associated with perception and learning. As the abstract truths are not "in" particular things, they are not the result of experience. A knowledge of them, therefore, must be nonexperiential or, put another way, *innate*.

What has been called the *problem of conduct* can be rephrased as a question: How should one live one's life? What is the right sort of life? Nested within such a question are vexing subsidiary questions. Thus: Why should one be good? What is "good"? Why should one's conduct be guided by any consideration other than pleasure or the avoidance of pain? Indeed, *is* one's conduct guided by any other consideration? Is there any guide to the right life other than custom and the values of one's own culture? Is the right sort of life for one person also right for others, or must each decide on an individual and personal basis? Who or what sets the standard in such matters? When cultural values conflict, how is one to decide which is right? In the realm of values, is anything finally "right" or "wrong," or is it all relative to the culture itself? Within the discipline of philosophy, such questions would give rise to the special fields of *ethics* and *moral philosophy*. But again, these same questions have come to define whole branches of psychological study: emotion and motivation as the sources of behavior; the role of reward and punishment in the control of behavior; the conditions favoring altruism; the social determinants of conduct; the formation of values and their role in life; the sources and nature of interpersonal influence; the nature of moral reasoning and the factors that influence it.

On these matters, too, Socrates' position, as conveyed in Plato's dialogues, changed somewhat over a course of years, but retained certain key elements that still engage the attention of philosophers and psychologists:

A. Human "psychic" nature is a complex or composite nature: part passionate, part volitional, part rational. Conduct is impelled by the emotions. Conduct also expresses what is willed or desired. Conduct also is answerable to certain judgments rationally reached. Thus, the "soul" is beset by antagonistic, even warring parties, not unlike a charioteer striving to reach a goal but pulled by two radically different horses; one tame and disciplined, the other wild and obstinate.

B. The right life, as with the right actions in a given circumstance, is one in which the ruling authority is that of *reason*, and where both emotion and the will are in the service of reason. The relationship among the three must be harmonious but ordered. Discord at this level is a disease; a species of madness for which only philosophical treatments are likely to succeed.

c. As with knowledge itself, the central rational principles of conduct—the ultimate dictates of right reason—are not visible and "out there," but within the person, needing careful cultivation and refinement. When this is achieved, one emerges as *virtuous*. Cultivation is by way of a rigorously controlled childhood, exposure to exemplary citizens, the removal of corrupting influences. Not many can achieve the desired end, for to do so requires certain native qualities that are essentially genetic in origin.

Finally, the *problem of governance*, as addressed in the dialogues, would begin to lay the foundations for the special field of political science and such subsidiary fields as philosophy of law (jurisprudence), political theory, comparative politics. Although these fields have been richly cultivated within philosophy and political science, they remain largely unattended by psychology, creating a great need for what might be called a *civic psychology*—the psychological aspects of life within an irreducibly *civic* context.

Plato's *Republic* offers the most developed expression of Socratic thought on the problem of governance, but it is a dialogue that begins not in an attempt to analyze the nature of the good state (*polis*), but the nature of the good man (*anthropos*). The latter needing to be enlarged in order to be seen more clearly, Socrates decides it is best to consider just what it is that makes the *polis* good. This will then offer a model by which to examine the nature of the good man. Note, then, that one of the foundational works in *political* science actually begins as in inquiry in *psychological* science. In keeping with the conclusions reached in the ethical and moral inquiries, the *Republic* defends the notion of a well ordered *polis* ruled by a "philosopher-king" whose just laws regulate the masses in precisely the way reason should shape and direct conduct for the individual. The vice of greed is to be eliminated by the elimination of personal property—even children are to be "owned" in common—and the guardians of the *polis* are to be produced by sound breeding policies (*eugenics*).

Aristotle and the Naturalistic Perspective

Clearly, Plato's dialogues cover nearly every issue that would come to instigate further study and debate in the various fields of philosophy, science, and psychology. Yet, in the form presented in the dialogues, so much is left to conversation, to (mere?) dispute—even to debating tricks of one sort or another—that posterity's debts to Plato are great, but mixed, and somewhat eccentric. There are other debts owed the ancient Greeks, however, especially the physicians of the ancient Greek world who attempted to account for mental and behavioral abnormalities in terms of physical disorders. The students and disciples of Hippocrates (c. 460–c. 377 B.C.) are especially noteworthy. In their commentaries on the Hippocratic approach to medicine they offered suggestive observations of the effects of brain disorders on perception, thought, and movement. They opposed the notion of "sacred" diseases (epilepsy), insisting that every disease should be understood in terms of bodily functions.

By far, however, the most direct debts to the ancient world are owed to Aristotle (384–322 B.C.), a physician's son and the greatest student Plato's Academy would claim. Where Plato's genius expresses itself in dialogues that might even be regarded as theater pieces, Aristotle's treatises are academic, systematic, progressive, detailed—the very qualities that mark out a field of inquiry as a *discipline*. In light of the way the term is correctly used, Aristotle is the first and among the greatest of psychologists; less a *philosopher's* psychologist than a *psychologist's* psychologist. Much of his theoretical work is based on direct observations designed to challenge what is merely speculative. His psychology is never far removed from the natural world in which biological and environmental influences operate. In his major works, the Platonic *psyche*—a disembodied repository of truths, present before the birth of the person and surviving death itself—is transformed into a set of actual powers and processes, tied directly to the life and adaptive potential of a living being.

As Aristotle employs the term, *psyche* is nothing but a principle—a grounding or first principle (*arche*) of living things (*zoon*). In the simplest forms of life the psychic power

---

ARISTOTLE (384–322 B.C.), a physician's son and sometime teacher of Alexander the Great, was the first and the greatest of ancient Greece's systematic thinkers. His separate treatises and studies were and remain foundational for the traditional scientific and humanistic subjects. Born in Stagirus on the coast of Thrace, at seventeen Aristotle was sent by his guardian, Proxenus (his father had died while he was a young boy), to Athens to complete his education. There he entered Plato's Academy, where he remained for twenty years. After Plato's death Aristotle left Athens and eventually landed at the court of Philip of Macedonia, becoming the tutor to the thirteen-year-old Alexander. On Philip's death he returned to Athens and set up his own school, the Lyceum; here he usually delivered lectures while walking, which led to his followers being labeled the "peripatetics." In Athens his connection with the conquering Alexander was, not surprisingly, a great advantage; but on Alexander's death in 323 B.C., a coup displaced Athens's pro-Macedonian government. Aristotle fled to Chalcis in Euboea, where he died within a year.

is expressed in the form of nutritive and reproductive functions. For any creature to be and to remain alive, it must have some means by which to obtain nutrition. For the species itself to continue, the same creature must have the power to procreate. At a level of greater complexity, psychic powers include the power of locomotion. Even plants move in the direction of the sun or, as in the case of the Venus flytrap, to enclose and digest an insect. At yet a greater level of complexity, to these powers of nutrition, procreation, and locomotion is added that of *sensation,* which, according to Aristotle, is central to the very definition of *animal.* An entity qualifies as animal insofar as it is capable of sensation. At still greater levels of complexity there is a power Aristotle refers to as intellectual, referring here to the ability to learn and remember based on experience. The animal kingdom displays all varieties of such ability. With the mature and healthy human being, however, there is a power added to all these that is special in its own right: the power or faculty of *reason (nous),* which is distinguishable from intelligence. By way of intelligence, a creature can learn and recall specifics. Reason, in the form of what Aristotle at one place calls *epistemonikon,* allows one to comprehend and to frame general and universal propositions. This is the power of genuinely abstract thought, which is the grounding not only of mathematics and logic but also of the rule of law. It is the power that allows human beings to give and to understand *reasons* for acting, and thus to be held responsible in light of abstract moral and juridical precepts. This focus on rational power is not, however, at the expense of perceptual sources of knowledge. In important respects, Aristotle is a commonsense psychologist, not skeptical about the functions of the senses, not dismissive of any power or process that is widely distributed within a given species.

The theory of human nature advanced by Aristotle is often referred to as *hylomorphic*, the roots here referring to the ancient Greek words for matter (*hule*) and form (*morphe*). The "soul," Aristotle argues, is "the form of the body." To understand the sense in which "form" is intended, it is useful to consider Aristotle's own example: If the soul were an eye, vision would be its form. Thus, the hand of a statue is "a hand in name only," for it does not perform the functions for which hands are intended or designed. Thus understood, a living thing is what it is *essentially* owing to a defining form of life or activity. It is in this sense that man is a rational animal; it is in this sense that something materially looking like a man but lacking all rational powers would be a man "in name only."

Aristotle developed a systematic psychology that included the biological, the social, and the political dimensions of life in such a way as to provide a full-scale theory of human nature. Within the general theory are special subsidiary theories of learning and memory, motivation and emotion, cognition and abstract thought; subsidiary theories anticipating developments in genetic psychology, sociobiology, gender studies. At the center of his psychological speculations is a more general *teleological* theory: The regular occurrences or features of the natural world are what they are for a purpose. Nature does not traffic in accidents but in lawful relationships. To understand any natural process, then, is to comprehend not merely the physical causes at work but that "final cause," the *that for the sake of which* the various links in the chain are formed. To identify man as a rational animal is to raise the fundamental question as to just what the rational powers are for; the end for which they were intended. Rationality here has the same status as, for example, the wings of a bird. The latter are present *for the sake of flight*. And rationality is present for the sake of . . . what? Aristotle's answer is that rational powers are employed in the service of securing a flourishing form of life, a life of happiness (*eudaimonia*), but where happiness is understood not as the sensuous pleasure of animals and children but the deep and enduring pleasure of a life rationally lived. Just how one goes about this task is a measure of that person's virtue or moral excellence (*arête*) and the basis on which that person answers to a certain *type*. Indeed, Aristotle's ethical writings, and his classic treatise *Rhetoric*, provide the foundations for theories of personality.

There is scarcely a topic that would come to give psychology greater definition over the course of centuries that was not addressed by Aristotle and for which Aristotle is not among the cited pioneers. To the extent that the subject itself is reducible to a definition, it would be the works of Aristotle that would yield the essential terms of the definition: *Psychology is the study of those perceptual, cognitive, and/or rational powers and processes by which organisms enter into relations with their physical and social environments in order to achieve ends determined by their specific natures.*

Philosophical Psychology after Aristotle

The development of psychology from its founding in ancient Greece to the seventeenth century is chiefly the work of (1) philosophers employing the method of introspection, who, consulting the nature of their own thoughts and actions, advanced general theories about the nature of mind and mental life; and (2) medical practitioners recording the effects of disease and injury on such psychological processes as perception, thought, memory, and movement. These centuries not only hosted some of the most inventive and agile minds of intellectual history, but also saw the founding of the modern university. Especially worthy of mention here are Saint Augustine (354–430), whose *Confessions* is a veritable treatise on psychological processes; Saint Thomas Aquinas (1225–1274), who remains one of the most discerning of the commentators on Aristotle and whose own original thought touched on the subjects of perception, cognition, and free will; and William of Ockham (1280–1349), who wrote at length on the cognitive basis of the concept of universals. By the twelfth century, the once modest abbey schools had been expanded to offer instruction in a variety of subjects, the school at Paris coming to have authentic status as a university featuring a curriculum in what would now be called the liberal arts.

From the middle of the seventeenth century, however, the possibility of a distinct *mental science* emerges as a realistic project. Three of the most influential figures in this development are René Descartes (1596–1650), Thomas Hobbes (1588–1679) and John Locke (1632–1704). The three are celebrated representatives of the great age of science that was the seventeenth century, the century of Kepler, Newton, Boyle, Galileo, Wren, Huygens. Descartes made significant contributions to mathematics and optics, earning the title of father of analytic geometry. Hobbes, after visiting the great Galileo and mastering the newly discovered laws and principles of mechanics, wrote a foundational treatise on human nature based on just such mechanistic principles. Locke, a fellow of the Royal Society and medical doctor, composed one of the most influential treatises in the history of philosophical psychology, *An Essay Concerning Human Understanding* (1690). It was an explicit attempt to develop a mental science along the lines of Newtonian science. On Locke's account, ideas are composites of more elementary sensations, held together as a result of associational forces. The mind is completely "furnished" by experience, its elementary sensations akin to Newtonian corpuscles, its associational laws functioning as a kind of gravitational force.

Although Descartes is known famously for a *dualistic*

theory, according to which mind is immaterial and utterly unlike any property of physical bodies, his psychological theories of perception, emotion, and motivation are utterly physiological at the level of explanation. Only the abstract rational powers of man are excluded from this scheme. Locke, though somewhat noncommittal, is clearly inclined to accept physiological processes as the grounding of all psychological processes, and Hobbes defends a radically *materialistic* psychology without reservation. In this productive age of philosophical psychology, therefore,

---

DESCARTES, RENÉ (1596–1650), was one of the geniuses of his age, a major contributor to mathematics, optics, and the biological sciences. His *Discourse on Method* and his *Meditations* established the "Cartesian" position on the nature of philosophical inquiry and the primacy of reason. Born near Tours, France, and educated at a Jesuit school, Descartes, like many of his contemporaries, came to believe in a strict separation of reason and faith. After spending much of his early life in Paris, in 1629 he went into seclusion in Holland for twenty years, jealously protecting his privacy by often changing residences. In 1649 he left Holland at the invitation of Queen Christina of Sweden to become her philosophy tutor. The uncongenial climate and early hours forced upon him by the queen led to his death soon after he arrived. Despite the theologically problematic implications of his philosophical work, Descartes never abandoned his Catholicism. At the time of his death his fame was such that many believed him to be a saint; by the time his body arrived back in France, relic-gatherers had been so many, and so enthusiastic, that his remains were considerably lighter.

the most influential works are those that mirror developments in the physical sciences and seek to pattern a scientific psychology along the same lines.

It is in the following century, that eighteenth century
of "Enlightenment," that Newtonian science reaches nearly
religious levels of discipleship. Advances in physics and
especially applied physics encourage and defend the con-
viction that no problem, no matter how complex, is im-
mune to the explanatory range of science. "Social engi-
neering" surfaces in the great works of the period, sometimes in the form of pamphlets and treatises, more power-
fully in the form of revolutionary rhetoric and upheaval.
The politics of the Enlightenment is largely a political psychology that would justify one mode of governance and
reject others on the grounds of a "correct" theory of human nature. With Locke, David Hume, and the other British empiricists, it is the *authority of experience* rather than
tradition or scripture that must settle matters of fact and
matters of principle. In the patrimony of Descartes, writ-
ers in the Enlightenment adopt an official skepticism before the claims of history, rejecting all that cannot be vin-
dicated in the arena of systematic observation and rational
analysis. Needless to say, life is more complicated than this,

and the various worlds of social and political life would (repeatedly) prove this Enlightenment "gospel" to be too thin by half.

It is in the same century that progress in medicine and more particularly in what would now be called neurology adds measurably to the thick book of clinical findings on the relationship between mind and body, brain and thought. By the end of the century Franz Gall (1758–1828), the father of *phrenology*, offers any number of compelling anatomical observations leading to the conclusion that specific psychological processes depend on specific regions of the cerebral cortex. The decades following these claims are devoted to testing them experimentally in order to establish where and to what extent specific psychological functions are located within the brain. Thus is the systematic study of *localization of function* launched, and thus does it continue to the present time.

PSYCHOLOGY AS SCIENCE

THERE IS NO sharply distinguishable period of time when psychology left its philosophical moorings and set sail independently. In point of fact, the very nature of the subject makes "independence" more a slogan than a reality. The development of a science, physics included, is based on any number of suppositions and orientations which are neither validated by the science nor contained within its own resources. Basic questions must be settled first (or seem to be settled), and only then can the inquiry begin. If, for example, physics is taken to be the study of matter and energy and the laws governing their behavior, then there must be some basis on which to defend this definition—some basis on which to identify a relationship as a *law*, an entity as *matter*, an influence as *energy*, etc. In a word, every special field of scientific inquiry has ineliminably *metaphysical* foundations, where "metaphysical" refers to the interrelated philosophical issues of *ontology* (the study or consideration of just *what there is* or what has *real being*) and *epistemology* (the critical examination of knowledge-claims and the means by which knowledge is acquired). There can be no science that is "independent" of these foundations, for it would be a gate swinging without hinges. There is, alas, a continuing blindness or resistance to this truism displayed by the vast majority of contemporary psychologists. There is, however, a different sense of "independent," and one that was invoked by many scientists in the nineteenth century eager to free their subjects from what they took to be merely philosophical squabbles. The most influential defenders of this sense of independence included Hermann von Helmholtz (1821–1894) in the German-speaking world, and John Stuart Mill (1806–1873) in England. Each in a different way set down the principles of experimental science, adapting these to the study of mental processes. Helmholtz grounded his theories in the physiological sciences. Mill resisted this, insisting that an experimental science concerned with the "laws of mind" could be prosecuted in a manner distinct from studies of the "laws of body." Both, however, were influential in creating a climate that nurtured the growth of a scientific and *experimental* psychology.

Among the pioneers of the new science were Wilhelm Wundt (1832–1920) at Leipzig and William James (1842–1910) at Harvard. Each established a laboratory within his university in which to study basic perceptual and mental processes. Priority is usually given to Wundt, whose Leipzig laboratory was established in the period 1878–1879, though James would note in his writings that his Harvard laboratory was up and running as early as 1875. But Wundt deserves priority on a basis more important than mere chronology. He founded a journal in which psychological find-ings could be published. He established graduate programs of study that would confer doctoral degrees on those who would then establish psychology programs at any number of universities in Europe, Great Britain, and the United States. Wundt in these respects is the modern "father" of experimental psychology, though William James's *Principles*

MILL, JOHN STUART (1806–1873), is generally considered to be the leading philosopher of the nineteenth century in the English-speak-ing world. His defenses of an empiricistic alternative to rationalism are authoritative and of enduring influence. In his logical works he developed formal principles of experimental science that continue to guide research strategies. The eldest son of philosopher James Mill, John Stuart's upbringing was, to say the least, intellectually rigorous; he knew Greek at age three, for example, and as a teenager, greatly influenced by the writings of Jeremy Bentham, he formed his own "utilitarian society." The extreme rigidity of his father's rearing methods probably caused Mill's mental breakdown, marked by severe depression, at age twenty-one. After recovering, his career took off. From 1823 to 1858, Mill worked for the British East India Company, rising from clerk to chief of the examiner's office. In 1851 he married the widow Mrs. Harriet Taylor, who had long been one of his intellectual companions, sometimes co-authoring articles with him. Mill served as a Member of Parliament from 1865 to 1868, winning the seat despite his refusal to spend any of his own money on the election (on the grounds that doing so would amount to buying his seat). Before his death in Avignon, Mill managed to write an enormous number of articles on a broad array of topics, the contents of which helped him to earn a reputation as a political progressive.

of Psychology (1890) would come to be its most developed expression. The character of this new science would be shaped by developments within the psychological domain but also and more importantly by two developments in more or less distinct domains. One of these was specific, the other by way of an accumulation. The specific development was Charles Darwin's (1809–1882) immensely influential works; the other, the work of many hands over a succession of decades. It is instructive to examine briefly how each of these was incorporated into the emerging discipline of psychology.

Darwinian Evolutionary Theory

Darwin's *Origin of Species* (1859), *Descent of Man* (1870) and *Expression of the Emotions in Animals and Man* (1871) came to dominate thinking in psychology nearly from the time of their initial publication. In defending a continuity theory of mental development, according to which human mental powers are mirrored throughout the animal kingdom, though to a lesser or altered degree, Darwin gave impetus and credibility to the study of the adaptive behavior of animals. Research programs addressed to instinctual behavior, mating and sexual selection, developmental processes from infancy to adulthood, species comparisons, studies of exceptional types—the full panoply—were to spring up seemingly overnight. Social institutions and practices now were to be understood in terms of selection pressures and challenges to survival. Racial comparisons were now framed in terms of relative degrees of evolution, with predictable and comforting racist explanations of socioeconomic strata. Mental illness was now understood in the language of adaptation. The long held thesis of *essentialism,* according to which a thing is what it is owing to an unchanging and essential aspect of its nature, now gave way to *contextualism,* according to which things adapt to the conditions under which they must struggle for survival. The overarching perspective was one that favored a form of psychological theory known as *functionalism*: The task of psychology is to establish the function of various psychological states and processes in the task of survival and successful adaptation. Instead of asking what is the essence of mind, the right question becomes, *What is the function of mental events?* It would become a central principal in William James's psychology that the one unfailing mark of the mental is action directed toward an end. James's student, E. L. Thorndike (1874–1949), expressed the same idea in the form of his famous *Law of Effect*: Behavior is more or less likely depending on the effects it produces. What functions to secure a satisfying state of affairs becomes ever more dominant; what leads to pain and suffering, ever less frequent.

Advances in Neurophysiology and Neurology

By 1800 there was evidence that muscles were activated by an electrical force, a theory at first contested but finally established early in the nineteenth century. Between 1810 (Sir Charles Bell) and 1822 (François Magendie) anatomical research revealed that the sensory and the motor functions of the nervous system were anatomically distinct. Information reaches the brain by way of sensory nerves entering the spinal cord on the dorsal surface; motor commands from the brain to the muscles exit from the spinal cord on the ventral surface.

Following the lead put in place by Gall—and his critics—research in the nineteenth century left no doubt whatever but that specific regions of the cerebral cortex, the cerebellum, the medulla, and deeper levels of the brain served specific functions. Paul Broca (1824–1880) discovered a lesion in the left frontal lobe in postmortem studies of the brain of his aphasic patient. *Broca's aphasia* left little doubt but that the crowning achievement of human psychological development—language—was a brain-based capacity. By the 1830s a coherent theory of reflex function had been developed by Marshall Hall and others. In the 1840s Helmholtz and others produced experimental data showing that the speed of nervous conduction—authoritatively regarded as almost infinitely rapid just a decade earlier—was a rather sluggish twenty to forty meters per second. Not long thereafter Emil Du Bois–Reymond (1818–1896) obtained evidence in support of the

---

WUNDT, WILHELM (1832–1920), is something of the "father" of modern experimental psychology, for it was Wundt who established the first academic laboratory devoted to psychological research (Leipzig, 1878–79), and the first journal in which such research could be published and widely distributed. His students were chosen by many leading universities eager to establish psychology departments on the "German" model. The son of a Lutheran clergyman, Wundt was born in the village of Nekarau, Germany. A physiologist by training, and a former assistant to Hermann von Helmholtz, Wundt taught the first academic course in psychology in 1862 at the University of Heidelberg. Much of Wundt's work focused on the senses. However, he was also concerned with identifying the "structure" or fundamental elements of consciousness through careful attention to conscious experience. Structuralism, as this mentalist approach to psychology is called, would later come to be rejected by American functionalists and behaviorists.

view that the electrical events in the nervous system were chemically created by a process now recognized as ionic. Step by step, the neurology clinic and the neurophysiology laboratory established ever firmer support for an essentially *physiological* psychology and for the "mental" being little more than a code word for what were finally chemical and physical processes. As would be repeated during the seasons of behavioristic psychology, the position here is characteristic of the "nothing but" fallacy mentioned in the introduction: The mind (life, love, virtue, etc.) should be understood as "nothing but" chemical, physical processes. A form of village credulity—never in short supply—is needed to adopt such a stance.

BEHAVIORISM

ONE ABIDING GOAL within the scientific community, at least since the nineteenth century, has been to demonstrate the ultimate unity of science. It was the aim of Ernst Mach (1838–1916) at the close of that century, and it was the aim of his intellectual descendants, the *logical positivists* of the 1930s. Although substantial disagreements can be found among the major figures in the movement, there was (and is) general agreement on these key points: First, that science is a distinct form of inquiry, its claims finally having to be settled at the level of relevant measurements and observations; second, that the subject matter of science is at least in principle *observable*, either directly or by way of observable effects; third, that the ultimate "stuff" of reality is *physical*—there is no ghostly stuff, mental or otherwise; finally, physics is not "metaphysics." No special place need be reserved for divine purposes or hidden designs. The first product of this perspective in psychology was the school of *behaviorism*, defended with great rhetorical flourishes in the works of John B. Watson. It received oblique support from the pioneering research on conditioned reflexes by Ivan Pavlov. And it was brought to its greatest conceptual maturity and influence by B. F. Skinner.

Evolutionary theory explains variation and stability in the characteristics of living things in terms of purely natural processes. Members of a given species display natural variations, some of these better equipping certain members to meet challenges to survival. In time, the naturally selected characteristics become more frequently represented within the breeding pool, the successful "types" becoming the common type. In the most general terms, behaviorism is predicated on the assumption that the same processes are at work at the level of adaptive behavior. Those responses that result in positive consequences become a more common feature of the organism's repertoire. Unsuccessful and maladaptive behavior is "extinguished."

It was Ivan Pavlov (1849–1936), the Russian physiologist who had won the Nobel Prize for research on digestion, who established the procedures by which to "condition" certain behavior to specific environmental stimuli. His research established that a basic biological reflex—salivation in response to food being placed in the mouth—could be brought under the control of a previously ineffective stimulus such as the ringing of a bell. The sequence, BELL-FOOD, repeated frequently would result in salivation to the sound of the bell, food no longer being required. This is the well-known paradigm of *classical (Pavlovian) conditioning*. Pavlov also showed that, once conditioned, a response such as salivation was elicited by a range of stimuli falling along the same continuum as that used to establish the conditioned response. Thus, once salivation is conditioned to a tone of 5000 Hz., the response will also be elicited by tones of 1000, 2000, 6000, etc. Under these conditions, Pavlov observed that the amount of salivation was progressively diminished as the test-stimuli became progressively less similar to the initial ("conditioned") stimulus. This common effect illustrates what is called *stimulus generalization*. With differential conditioning— for example, where during conditioning food is paired with a given tone but where other tones are presented without food—the conditioned response is more sharply "tuned" to the value of the conditioned stimulus, illustrating the process of *stimulus discrimination*.

JAMES, WILLIAM (1842–1910), was America's greatest philosopher and most incisive psychologist. His *Principles of Psychology* remains a landmark in the field. In 1875 James introduced experimental psychology at Harvard University, establishing what was probably the first academic psychology laboratory in the United States. The brother of novelist Henry James, William was born in New York City in 1842. After abandoning an early love for painting, James entered the Harvard School of Medicine in 1864. He received his M.D. in 1869 but at the same time was overcome by a bout of severe depression. Finally in 1872 he began to teach physiology courses to undergraduates at Harvard, eventually moving on to teach courses in psychology and philosophy. In 1898 he first identified himself in print as a pragmatist, the school of thought with which he is now most often associated. But his interests ranged widely, and he was unique among his contemporary colleagues in the emerging field of psychology for his genuine openness to questions concerning religion and the supernatural. This latter interest led to an invitation to deliver the Gifford lectures at the University of Edinburgh in 1901. These lectures were published the next year as *Varieties of Religious Experience,* which remains a classic. He died of heart failure in 1910.

Daniel N. Robinson

Pavlov theorized that these behavioral effects reflected processes occurring in the cerebral cortex of the animal. His was a radically physiological theory of conditioning. In America, John B. Watson (1878–1958) launched a relentless defense of an essentially behavioristic psychology, which downplayed the specific physiological processes proposed by Pavlov but otherwise took Pavlov's findings as supportive of a purely behavioristic school of psychology. Behaviorism is committed to the study of observable behavior, making no assumptions about the operation or even the existence of a "mind" or "mental" events on which the behavior allegedly depends. The rationale is that the subject matter of science is what is observable. One can observe the behavior of others, not their minds. With few exceptions, behaviorism is opposed to *mentalism*, this term referring to theories that explain behavior as the result of mental events and processes.

Owing to the influential writing of B. F. Skinner (1904–1990), behaviorism also was long opposed to explanations of adaptive behavior based on physiological processes or events in the brain. It was a central precept within behaviorism, as B. F. Skinner would have behaviorism understood, that a purely descriptive science of behavior was under no obligation to locate the internal processes or mechanisms associated with adaptive behavior. The facts of behavior are just *there* to be observed; their factual standing is unaltered by observations made at some other (e.g., physiological, genetic, anatomical) level of observation. In keeping with this perspective, behavioristic psychologists locate the factors shaping or controlling behavior in the environment external to the organism rather than in that inner environment of such interest to biologists. Hence, critics of behaviorism often labeled it the psychology of "the empty organism."

NEUROPSYCHOLOGY AND COGNITIVE NEUROSCIENCE

A BEHAVIORAL SCIENCE need not be indifferent to internal states and processes. Largely through the very refinements in behavioral measurement and control achieved by behavioristic psychologists, it became possible, from the 1950s and thereafter, to examine the physiological and biochemical substrates of highly specific aspects of perception, learning, motivation, emotion, and social interaction. As of the new millennium, it can be said that the most active and expanding field in psychology is that of *cognitive neuroscience,* which comprises specialists in experimental psychology, computer science, neurology and neurophysiology, artificial intelligence, and philosophy of mind.

One of the foundations of cognitive neuroscience is the specialty of *neuropsychology.* Over the decades, the subject of this specialty has been subsumed under different headings: physiological psychology, psychobiology, biological psychology, medical psychology. Sharp distinctions cannot be made here. In general terms, however, both neuropsychology and medical psychology have been concerned chiefly with the functions of the human nervous system in

---

DARWIN, CHARLES (1809–1882), studied for careers in medicine and theology at the University of Edinburgh and Cambridge University, respectfully, but neither could maintain his interest. Rather, he committed himself early to the study of natural phenomena, earning the (unpaid) position of naturalist on the HMS *Beagle,* a ship headed for an exploratory trip along the Pacific coast of South America (1831–36). Its voyages supplied Darwin with the data that would eventually be incorporated into his landmark *Origin of Species,* published in 1859. In the intervening years Darwin married, fathered nine children, made a name for himself in the scientific community as a naturalist, wrote a popular account of his travels on the *Beagle,* and began reading the work of Thomas Malthus. *The Origin of Species* was concerned almost exclusively with evolution in the nonhuman world, but in *The Descent of Man* (1871) Darwin applied his theory of evolution by natural selection to man.

health and disease. Physiological psychology, psychobiology, and biological psychology are less specifically concerned with human beings and more broadly devoted to studies of nonhuman animals. What research and theory in all these areas—under all of these headings—have in common are relationships between psychological processes or capacities or abilities and specific neurophysiological, neurochemical, and neuroanatomical substrates.

As noted above, observations of this sort appear as early as the Hippocratic school of medicine in ancient Greece. Only after centuries of study, often interrupted by silent periods lasting still more centuries, were accurate anatomies of human and nonhuman nervous systems discovered and recorded. Not only did details await the discovery of the microscope in the seventeenth century, but the actual mode of function of the nervous system awaited the discovery of instruments by which to record electrical events. Only in the twentieth century was there firm proof of the existence of structurally independent *neurons*, the cellular units of the nervous system. Only in the twentieth century was there firm proof that the mode of transmission of information from one neuron to another is by way of chemical *transmitters*.

The twentieth century began with anatomical evidence of neuronal specialization; it ended with computational and visualization techniques capable of displaying in real time the actual activity in various structures throughout the entire brain. Combined with systematic studies in clinical neurology, the developed "brain sciences" now are able to identify, often at the cellular level, those processes and events reliably associated with the full range of perceptual, cognitive, behavioral, motivational and emotional aspects of human and nonhuman animal psychology. That science of phrenology that had been launched by Gall at the end of the eighteenth century has evolved in ways perhaps only he would have imagined at the time.

The emergence of cognitive neuroscience has been gradual. Its foundations were laid by basic research in sensory and perceptual processes: studies of sensory threshold, attention, information processing, target recognition, short-term memory, etc. Decades of basic research in these fields led to the modeling of mental functions as a set of *modules* of this general type:

1. Impinging stimuli initiate responses in the sensory organs.

2. The sensory response electrically "codes" such features

of the stimulus as intensity, size, location.

3. The coded signals are stored briefly where they can be compared with previously stored information.

4. Comparisons and weighting determine whether the new information is retained or erased.

5. Retained information is given weights as a result of those emotional or motivational processes with which they are associated.

6. Outputs from memory stores initiate processes associated with behavior.

7. The moment-to-moment consequences of behavior are reported back to the system by way of feedback circuits, thus providing something of a closed-loop ("servomechanistic") device capable of adapting to changing conditions.

This is a simple and clearly incomplete sketch of some of the "modules" presumed to operate as animals and persons face one or another environmental challenge. Theories based on this sort of model seek support from studies of the effects of brain lesions, selective stimulation and recording from specific brain sites, and postmortem studies of patients known to have suffered from one or another psychological deficit.

Many leading figures in the field of cognitive neuroscience have adopted theories of this sort. Complex psychological processes are assumed to arise from the activation of more elementary processes. "Problem-solving" on this account is a term that actually covers a range of distinguishable functions: selective attention, sensory coding, perceptual registration, memory, motivational and emotional "gain" or amplification, recruitment of instinctual or acquired behavioral adjustments. These separate functions are thought by many to depend on various functional *modules* within the brain, interconnected by specific pathways and integrated in different ways to solve different classes of problems.

Despite the enthusiasm with which such theories have been advanced and defended, it should be noted that there is no clear understanding of just what it is about an anatomical structure—a collection of cells—that makes it a "module," nor is it at all clear that calling such cells a "memory module" is even intelligible. It is the *person* or *animal* who remembers the left and right turns in the maze. This much is clear. However, to claim that some structure in the brain "remembers" is, to say no more, surely less than clear. The rationale or motive behind such expressions arises from the "unity of sciences" perspective which, in its more popular form, seeks *reductionistic* explanations. The aim is to explain complex events by reducing them to a set of simpler or more elementary events, in much the way that the properties of water might be reduced to those of hydrogen and oxygen in the appropriate combination. The value of this approach, its defenders would contend, is that it replaces subjective and ambiguous accounts with explanations based on objective scientific principles. There are, however, a number of compelling reasons for resisting reductionism:

PAVLOV, IVAN (1849–1936), the Nobel Prize–winning Russian physiologist, established the principles of classical conditioning. These principles grounded the philosophical theory of "associations" in the actual physiology of the nervous system. Pavlovian psychology was a form of behavioristic psychology, to be replaced by the quite different "Skinnerian" version. Born in central Russia in the village of Ryazan, and the son of an Orthodox priest, Pavlov was originally intended for the priesthood, but, like Darwin—indeed, partly because of Darwin—he decided to pursue a scientific career instead. At the University of St. Petersburg he studied chemistry and physiology, receiving his doctorate in 1879. Pavlov did not set out to contribute to psychology; the experiments that made him famous began as studies of digestion, which was the topic of research for which he won the Nobel Prize in 1904, and he was dubious about the new discipline of psychiatry. A sometime outspoken critic of the Soviet government after the October Revolution, his worldwide fame and usefulness to the Communist Party as an exemplar of its scientific progressivism kept him from persecution until his death at the age of eighty-seven.

1.   Attempts to reduce psychological phenomena to physiological events are likely to result not in the explanation but in the elimination of the very phenomena of interest. For example, to reduce the experience of color to discharge patterns in neurons and brain cells is to capture nothing that gives the experience its felt and immediately known quality.

2. There is a somewhat self-defeating feature in reductionistic schemes. After all, what makes events in the nervous system of interest to psychologists is the reliability with which these events are associated with, alas, *psychological* events and processes. To seek to eliminate these is to seek to eliminate just what it is that gives the nervous system its importance within psychology.

3. The very concept of an *explanation* is understood in radically different ways in various contexts. The victim of a fatal shooting died (a) owing to wounds and loss of blood, (b) because he was known by his assailant as in possession of a large amount of money, (c) because the money in question had been stolen from the assailant and (d) because the assailant was being blackmailed by the mob. There is no basis on which to declare (a) the best explanation simply because it is based on "objective scientific principles."

4. There are still good reasons for assuming that the very logic of scientific inquiry and explanation, as it has been developed in physics, is finally inapplicable to the range of events (cultural, aesthetic, moral, judicial, political, interpersonal) that constitute the very content of psychology. Thus, reductionistic strategies are not merely premature but finally misguided.

FREUD AND DEPTH PSYCHOLOGY
~

IT IS OFTEN OVERLOOKED that the widespread influence of "Freudian" psychology arose from the work of a clinical neurologist, practicing in Vienna at the close of the nineteenth century, and having as his main objective a clearer understanding of the causes of certain "hysterical" symptoms. Sigmund Freud (1856–1939), like Darwin, did not intend to change the world of thought. What he discovered in his clinical practice was a relationship between certain symptoms (paralyses, blindness, severe anxiety) and the *repression* of psychologically disturbing thoughts or past experiences. In the manner of the conservation laws in physics (which had been discovered in Freud's lifetime), there seemed to be a *psychic* energy that was also "conserved," but able to express itself in various ways. Thus, the hysterical symptom could be regarded as the *physical* manifestation of a process of *psychic* repression.

By 1900 Freud would borrow liberally from the evolutionary theory that was now generally accepted by the scientific community. Darwin offered strong arguments in support of the claim that the psychological aspects of man fell along the same continuum as that containing the mental life of nonhuman animals. Freud accepted the notion that survival-instincts impel human actions in a manner widely displayed in the animal kingdom. Nature equips animals to find pleasure in what finally determines the survival of the individual animal and its species. The suckling infant is motivated not by considerations of nutrition but by sheer sensual pleasure. Thus did Freud offer a theory of *psychosexual development*, marking out the stages, from infancy to adulthood, of dominant patterns of sexual activity. The culminating stage is that of *heterosexual procreative sexuality*, the means by which the species is preserved.

The central theoretical element in Freudian psychology is that of *unconscious motivation*. The reasons persons give for their actions may well be impelled by unconscious desires that would lead to social ostracism were they publicized. In the course of *socialization*, the developing child, naturally inclined toward self-gratification and otherwise obedient to the *pleasure principle*, comes face-to-face with that *reality principle* imposed by adult society. The conflict between these competing principles is lifelong. Total domination by the reality principle results in a less than authentic life; total yielding to the pleasure principle renders one unfit for life within society.

Because the sources of desire and action are (allegedly) *unconscious*, the person is unable to understand at the deeper and most informing levels just why his or her aims and frustrations, triumphs and failures take the turn they do. The psychological disturbances that plague the adult are, according to the theory, first planted in childhood, surviving now as what Freud called a "childhood remnant." It is only through a process of *depth analysis* that the patient can be returned to the very time when the seeds of the conflict were sewn. It is the analyst, not the patient, who finds the deeper meaning and significance in the patient's anxieties, hopes, failures.

The Freudian perspective is so broad in its expression as to be by now resistant to clear definition. It is a perspective that has influenced philosophy, literary criticism, law, the arts, and yes, even psychology! It may be that psychology is now less influenced than the others. As for the influences, perhaps the most general are these:

1. A skepticism toward rational explanations of individual actions and cultural values. On the psychoanalytic understanding as Freud developed it, rational accounts typically are *rationalizations*, designed to put in a favorable light initiatives and practices actually driven by animalistic motives of the Darwinian stripe. Darwin + Freud = (much of) evolutionary psychology and sociobiology.

2. A relativism in the matter of basic moral precepts. "Morality" on the psychoanalytic account is a set of concessions that the pleasure principle must make to the reality principle if unacceptable degrees of censure and punishment are to be avoided. There are no absolutes in the moral sphere, reached by reason and valid in all contexts; only the daily collision between ego and world, primal urges and their repression, primal urges and their symbolic transformations.

3. A species of psychological determinism. The fixity of the stages of psychosexual development, the iron nature of evolutionary forces and laws, and the requirements imposed by civilization all work to render the individual life

one of discontent, conflict, quiet desperation. This is all "in the cards," so to speak, with amelioration in the form of a resigned understanding achieved through depth analysis.

It was Freud's own expectation, variously affirmed and questioned, that the psychoanalytic terms and principles would ultimately be recast as facts within a developed science of neurophysiology. His ultimate objective was the biologizing of the mind, with psychoanalytic theory being but a first step. However, the theory itself is essentially a kind of *narrative* with little by way of the testable, the measurable—in a word, the scientifically knowable. It is something of a story about human nature; something of a gothic novel which many find to be eerie, and many others just *true*—as in "true to my life."

So much ink has been spilled in defense and in defiance of Freud's writings that little would be gained by adding to either side of the ledger here. The actual practice of psychotherapy, as reported by therapists themselves, is only loosely indebted to Freud and derives nothing from the theory by way of a "how to" guide to diagnosis and treatment. The Darwinian elements are neither more nor less compelling in Freudian thought than in Darwin's own or, for that matter, in current books and articles that treat these elements as gospel. The recognition that should guide students confronting Freudian theory for the first time is that, as a "theory," it scarcely measures up to what one demands of scientific theories; moreover, that it is in the very nature of Freudian "theory" to be adaptable to nearly any evidence that might be arrayed against it. Perhaps it is best understood as a richly imaginative account of human nature, as one might find in especially probing works of fiction.

THE SOCIAL CONTEXT

IF ONE CONSIDERS the three dominant "deterministic" perspectives in psychology—the behavioristic, the neuropsychological, and the genetic—it becomes clear that each and all must find a daunting challenge in many of the findings in social psychology. Studies of bystander-effects, of mock prisons, of peer pressure, of obedience, all point to the power of the immediate context on behavior and judgment. The famous and controversial research of Stanley Milgram (1933–1984) required volunteers to deliver what they had reason to believe were painful and potentially lethal shocks to human subjects in experiments (falsely) described as studies of the role of punishment in learning and memory. Approximately two-thirds of the subjects ("teachers") in the study continued to increase what they were told was the voltage of shocks delivered to "learners" who were actually collaborators in the research. As the latter feigned pain and suffering, no more than a bit of encouragement from laboratory assistants was needed to keep the "teachers" obedient to the aims of the research. Comparable

---

Watson, John B. (1878–1958), was the "father" of modern behaviorism. His lectures and writing were directed toward a relentless defense of an objective science of psychology, one that would take observable behavior as the discipline's sole subject matter. His "Psychology as the Behaviorist Views it," which appeared in *Psychological Review* in 1913, was a rallying call to an entire generation of psychologists. Born near Greenville, South Carolina, Watson received his B.A. and M.A. degrees from Furman University. At twenty-two, he entered graduate school at the University of Chicago, where he was strongly influenced by the pragmatist-functionalist ideas of Chicago professors John Dewey, George Herbert Mead, and James Rowland Angell, and where he began to develop his behaviorist theory. In 1908 he moved to Johns Hopkins University as a full professor, and five years later launched his attack on mainstream psychology. A man equipped with the instincts and drive of a missionary, Watson published in 1919 a popular introductory textbook that played a large role in advancing his theory. Like his disciple B. F. Skinner, he hoped his work would spur widespread social reorganization. In 1920 he was forced to resign from Johns Hopkins after his wife and former graduate student initiated divorce proceedings. He spent the rest of his career as an advertising executive in New York.

effects were obtained by Philip Zimbardo (b. 1933) in studies that simulated the conditions of imprisonment. Randomly assigned to the category of "prisoner" or "guard," Stanford students participated in research that called upon some of them, in their assigned capacity of uniformed guards, to maintain order among the prisoners. In a matter of days the student-guards displayed sadistic conduct toward now clearly submissive "prisoners," many of whom were willing to betray their peers for an extra blanket or sign of approval.

What is profoundly suggestive about such research is the degree to which a veritable lifetime of reinforcement for decent behavior is seemingly undone by contextual factors involving pressures toward conformity. But profoundly missing in discussions of such findings are reflections on that reliable minority that resists such pressures and retains a fidelity to worthy principles. It is not too much to propose that the truly interesting subjects in research of this sort are those more or less ignored, as attention is heaped on the ever-pliant majority.

Experiments in social psychology often reflect a highly realistic quality generally missing in laboratory investigations in psychology. The subjects in a social psychology study are often placed in realistic settings or are asked how they would respond in such settings. The settings, often contrived with remarkable inventiveness, have permitted studies of prejudice, self-appraisal, the strong inclination toward consistency, vulnerability to external presssures, etc. Over the decades of such research yet another conception of human nature has been crafted; one in which the sources or causes of significant actions may well be different from the explanations the actual actors give. Although not psy-

---

SKINNER, B. F. (1904–1990), was, with the exception of Sigmund Freud, the most influential psychologist of the twentieth century. His studies of conditioning and learning in rats and pigeons came to be veritable models of the most complex human activities, including wagers and gambling, child rearing, interpersonal relations, war itself! After majoring in literature at Hamilton College, Skinner moved to New York City to pursue a writing career. This having failed, he removed to Harvard University, where he took his Ph.D. in 1931. In 1936 he took up academic residence at the University of Minnesota, and there, building on the work of John Watson, began to develop his influential, and often controversial, behaviorist theory. His novel, *Walden Two* (1948), depicted the creation of a utopian society based on behaviorist principles. Skinner was not afraid to subject his own family members to such principles: his second daughter spent much of her infancy in his "baby box," a device that allowed him to strictly control environmental influences on her development. After a brief stint at Indiana University, Skinner ended up at Harvard in 1948, where he remained for the rest of his career. In 1971 he published *Beyond Freedom and Dignity,* a volume of political and social thought whose title speaks volumes about the implications of Skinnerian psychology.

choanalytic in nature, this conception of human nature again focuses on determinants of action and perception falling beyond the conscious control or awareness of persons. Of course, this conception is based on trends violated at least some of the time by some subjects. Moreover, it is often the case that the very framing of the context or the social dilemma restricts participants to a far greater extent than one would find in the real world. The importance of the research and theory is that it provides vivid reminders of the conditions that might disarm persons and find them doing things which, on reflection and in a composed state, they would avoid.

HUMAN DEVELOPMENT:
MORAL AND CIVIC

IMAGINATIVE AND SYSTEMATIC research conducted in the past half-century leaves no doubt but that infants enter the world with highly developed perceptual capacities and more than the rudiments of cognitive, problem-solving processes. It is also clear that, from the earliest stages of vocalization, the very young child is, as it were, *speaking*—which is to say emitting vocalizations according to basic rules—and that it is this language that adult language comes to replace. The child is, indeed, a "little linguist."

Controversy still surrounds the question of those nurturing conditions that are essential to normal psychological development. Laboratory research with nonhuman animals, for all the attention paid to it, has actually settled none of this. Perhaps the most influential program of such research was that conducted by Harry F. Harlow (1905–1981), who deprived infant rhesus monkeys of access to their mothers, allowing them only to cuddle up to cloth or wire dolls. Harlow's findings indicated that severe maladjustment was a reliable consequence of such deprivation, partly reduced in those animals having at least a doll to attach themselves to.

Needless to say, no such research was required to inform intelligent persons that children removed from all human contact from the earliest stages of life would more than likely acquire maladaptive modes of behavior. But a knowledge of the destructive consequences of extreme deprivation offers no information whatever as to the essential conditions for a normal and flourishing course of development. The thick literature of biography and autobiography is sufficient to establish that no fixed formula is available here. Persons have failed miserably in life even after a privileged childhood of love and care; others have achieved utterly successful and rewarding lives after a childhood of misery and abuse. Thus, there is no iron law establishing the dos and don'ts of childrearing. There is, however, a common sense fortified by a knowledge of the ingredients often found in the developmental histories of those whose lives are worthy of emulation and respect.

It was a fixture in the philosophical and psychological treatises of the ancient Greek and Roman worlds that children are to be reared for *citizenship*, and that this required systematic schooling in what is often translated as *virtue*. The Greek *arête* translates readily as *moral excellence* and refers to a set of behavioral and emotional dispositions, powers of self-control, and the adoption of worthy goals. At the peak of its civilization, Rome instituted methods of education that included in the curriculum dress codes, posture, tone of voice, rhetorical skills, and, of course, the "martial arts." Clearly, the manner in which children are reared for civic life will reflect the form of civic life adopted by the larger culture. Rome did not exist for its citizens; they lived for the glory of Rome. In the Western democracies, based on respect for the dignity of the individual and committed to preserving the basic liberties of the individual, a different regimen or curriculum is required; but there is now not great agreement on what that should include. Nor is there much activity within psychology devoted to the question.

To the extent that there is a *psychology of moral development*, it is partitioned into a small part of the field of *cognitive psychology* and a comparably modest portion of the field of *social psychology*. With cognitive psychology, there

---

FREUD, SIGMUND (1856–1939), began his professional career as a practicing neurologist. His encounter with the "hysterical" symptoms of neurotic patients led him to study the use of hypnosis as a diagnostic and therapeutic approach. He was then led to that theory of repression that is foundational for the entire "Freudian" psychology of mental illness. Born in Freiberg, Moravia, Freud's family moved to Vienna when he was four; he would remain in that city until forced to leave by the Nazis in 1937. His volatile and unhappy marriage commenced in 1886, the same year in which he set up his private practice in the treatment of psychiatric problems. In formulating his theories Freud was heavily influenced by the work of French neurologist Jean Charcot and his colleague in Vienna, Josef Breuer (with whom, as with almost all his colleagues and students, he would later have a falling out). Freud did not gain wide public attention until 1908–09, when the first International Psychoanalytic Congress was held and he traveled to the United States to deliver a series of lectures. The father of six, including daughter Anna, who later also became a well-known psychoanalyst, Freud died of cancer in England in 1939.

is a long but spotty history of interest in how children come to comprehend moral problems and the basis on which they reach solutions. The early work was done by Jean Piaget (1896–1980), who employed the method of storytelling. Thus: A man's wife is deathly ill and needs medication. The nearest pharmacy has the medicine but is charging a price vastly greater than the husband can afford, refusing to give it to him unless he pays. The husband waits till the pharmacy closes for the day, then breaks in, steals the medicine, and returns home with it to save his wife's life. Did the husband do the right thing? If so, why? If not, why not? If he is caught, should he be punished? Etc.

Piaget discovered that the very young child solves all such problems in terms of the consequences of an action: If it is punished, it is wrong; if rewarded, it is right. Older children and young adults judge the morality of actions not in terms of how others react to them but in terms of principles personally adopted. Piaget distinguished the two cognitive periods as *heteronomous* (Greek *hetero* = other; *nomos* = law) and *autonomous* (Greek *auto* = self); those whose moral laws or rules are imposed by others are said to be in the heteronomous period, and those who are self-ruling are said to be in the autonomous period. Building on Piaget's work years later, Lawrence Kohlberg (1927–1987) studied a wide range of age groups in various cultures and advanced a multi-state theory of moral development. It is a precept within Kohlberg's theory that the stages must be passed through successively and that, though the stages are related to age, age alone is no guarantee of refined moral judgment.

Many social psychology studies, as noted above, have considered the conditions under which persons behave altruistically; the conditions that incline persons to deceive others; the conditions under which even basic principles seem vulnerable to peer pressure or the demand character-istics of the "situation." Whereas the Piagetian and Kohlbergian approaches consider cognitive processes gen-erating moral judgments, social psychologists tend to con-sider the social aims persons seek to achieve by judging or acting in certain ways. Thus, whether or not one comes to the aid of others in distress depends to some extent on whether anyone else is present and, if present, whether that other person is inclined to get involved. There is, it seems, a difference between how in cognitive terms one *judges* when and whether altruism is called for, and if, in the actual situation, one *acts* altruistically. Beyond these generalities, psychology at present offers little guidance or even a plan of research on such a central issue as civic development.

ABIDING ISSUES: AN EPILOGUE
❧

As should be clear, psychology as a discipline of study and research might well include the full range of human endeavors at the level of the individual person, the social collective, and even national groups. It cannot be a fault of psychology that it is unable to shed bright light on all such endeavors. Less than two centuries old as an independent field of experimental science, psychology continues to refine its methods and, to a lesser extent, its overall perspective on just what topics are to be central to its mission. At present, the overall perspective is still method-bound. That is, psychology as it appears in the major texts and major academic departments is committed to methods of inquiry that, by their nature, dictate the problems to be addressed. This is a backward arrangement. Rather, certain problems and issues should be chosen as in some sense "right" for the discipline, followed by the development of methods suited to just these problems and issues.

Committed to laboratory study and statistical modes

of description and analysis, psychology continues to have trouble with actual individual persons, individual minds setting out to achieve goals that are personal, arising from motives that may be quirky, and guided by considerations that are various and shifting. Rather, the approved methods offer fairly reliable statistical descriptions of data drawn from collectives and pooled in such a way as to wash out individuality itself. In striving to be a science of *everyone,* it is unable to say much of consequence about *anyone.*

Then, too, the three domains in which the psychological side of human life expresses itself most vividly— the civic (political), the aesthetic, and the abstract—have been grossly neglected, presumably because the official "methodology" is unable to adapt itself to such matters. There is no political psychology as such; just a rag-tag collection of ad hoc studies on, e.g., voting behavior. There is no aesthetic psychology as such; just some work on what persons perceive and appreciate in, e.g., paintings or music. And, for all the talk of a "cognitive revolution," there is little within the discipline that explores the relationship between abstract thought and, e.g., principles of justice and fairness.

There is much to be done!

Daniel N. Robinson

FURTHER READING

❦

Aristotle, *On the Soul.* This is the earliest systematic treatment of the psychological functions observed in the plant and animal kingdoms.

Charles Darwin, *The Descent of Man* (London, J. Murray, 1871). In this work, Darwin applies evolutionary principles to human psychology and defends the claim that human mental functions vary in degree, rather than kind, when compared with nonhuman animals.

Daniel Dennett, *Brainstorms: Philosophical Essays on Mind and Psychology* (Montgomery, Vt.: Bradford Books, 1978). This collection of essays presents Daniel Dennett's always interesting conceptions of "mental" processes as these can be considered in light of artificial intelligence and computational principles.

Sigmund Freud, *Über Psychoanalyse: fünf Vorlesungen, gehalten zer 20jährigen Gründungsfeier der Clark University in Worcester, Mass., September 1909,* published in English as *The Origin and Development of Psychoanalysis* (Chicago: Gateway Editions, 1955). These were the lectures delivered at Clark University, bringing to the attention of a wide American audience the central tenets of Freudian psychology.

William James, *The Principles of Psychology* (New York: H. Holt, 1890). This is the "gold standard" of texts in general psychology, composed by America's greatest philosopher.

Derek Parfit, *Reasons and Persons* (Oxford: Clarendon Press, 1984). Parfit takes up the long vexed question of "personal identity": How there can be a stable "person" amidst the bodily changes that occur moment to moment. His analysis leads him to conclude that the concept of an enduring "self" is untenable.

Wilder Penfield, *The Mystery of the Mind: A Critical Study of Consciousness and the Human Brain* (Princeton, N.J.: Princeton University Press, 1975). One of the greatest neurosurgeons of modern times, Penfield here summarize the experiences of a lifetime in observing the living human brains of patients. He is left with the conclusion that, apart from the complex biology of brain function, there is a genuinely *mental* reality that cannot be explained in physical terms.

Roger Penrose, *The Emperor's New Mind: Concerning Computers, Minds, and the Laws of Physics* (Oxford: Oxford University Press, 1985). In this important but very difficult work, Roger Penrose develops formal arguments against the thesis that mental events can be mimicked by computational devices, no matter how powerful.

Daniel N. Robinson, *An Intellectual History of Psychology* (New York: Macmillan, 1976). A survey of major conjectures on the nature of psychology from the pre-Socratic philosophers to contemporary cognitive neuroscience. Also, *The Mind: An Oxford Reader,* ed. Daniel N. Robinson (Oxford: Oxford University Press, 1998). Conveniently placed within one volume and supplemented with lengthy introductions, major works on mind and brain are presented. Ancient and modern sources are included.

John Sabini and Maury Silver, *Moralities of Everyday Life* (Oxford: Oxford University Press, 1982). Against traditional philosophical theories of morality, Sabini and Silver summarize research on the manner in which persons in actual settings judge the moral dimensions of the situation.

Oliver Sacks, *The Man Who Mistook His Wife for a Hat and Other Clinical Tales* (New York: Summit Books, 1985). Dr. Sacks presents a rich variety of cases from the neuropsychiatric clinic, illustrating the extraordinary range of symptoms arising from insults to the brain.

B. F. Skinner, *Science and Human Behavior* (New York: Macmillan, 1953). This is one of the most influential defenses of a behavioristic approach to psychology, written by the most influential behaviorist.

Robert Sternberg, ed. *The Nature of Cognition* (Cambridge, Mass.: MIT Press, 1999). In this volume one finds the data and the theories that helped launch the "cognitive revolution."

EMBARKING ON A LIFELONG PURSUIT OF KNOWLEDGE?

*Take Advantage of These New Resources
& a New Website*

The ISI Guides to the Major Disciplines are part of the Intercollegiate Studies Institute's (ISI) **Student Self-Reliance Project**, an integrated, sequential program of educational supplements designed to guide students in making key decisions that will enable them to acquire an appreciation of the accomplishments of Western civilization.

Developed with fifteen months of detailed advice from college professors and students, these resources provide advice in course selection and guidance in actual coursework. The project elements can be used independently by students to navigate the existing university curriculum in a way that deepens their understanding of our Western intellectual heritage. As indicated below, the Project's integrated components will answer key questions at each stage of a student's education.

What are the strengths and weaknesses of the most selective schools?
Choosing the Right College directs prospective college students to the best and worst that top American colleges have to offer.

What is the essence of a liberal arts education?
A Student's Guide to Liberal Learning introduces students to the vital connection between liberal education and political liberty.

What core courses should every student take?

A Student's Guide to the Core Curriculum instructs students in building their own core curricula, utilizing electives available at virtually every university, and discusses how to identify and overcome contemporary political biases in those courses.

How can students learn from the best minds in their major fields of study?

Student Guides to the Major Disciplines introduce students to overlooked and misrepresented classics, facilitating work within their majors. Guides currently available assess the fields of literature, philosophy, U.S. history, economics, political philosophy, and the study of history generally.

Which great modern thinkers are neglected?

The Library of Modern Thinkers introduces students to great minds who have contributed to the literature of the West and who are neglected or denigrated in today's classroom. Figures in this series include Robert Nisbet, Eric Voegelin, Wilhelm Röpke, Ludwig von Mises, Michael Oakeshott, Andrew Nelson Lytle, Bertrand de Jouvenel, and others.

In order to address the academic problems faced by every student in an ongoing manner, a new website, **www.collegeguide.org**, was recently launched. It offers easy access to unparalleled resources for making the most of one's college experience, and it features an interactive component that will allow students to pose questions about academic life on America's college campuses.

These features make ISI a one-stop organization for serious students of all ages. Visit **www.isi.org** or call **1-800-526-7022** and consider adding your name to the 50,000-plus ISI membership list of teachers, students, and professors.